A Boating Life
Adventures of a tiller girl

by Jane Pollard

A Boating Life: Adventures of a tiller girl

ISBN: 978-1-910181-88-1

Author Jane Pollard, March 2021
Published and Printed by Anchorprint Group Ltd.

Copyright © Jane Pollard
All rights reserved.

No part of this publication may be reproduced, stored in a retrieval system, transmitted or utilised in any form or by any means, electronic, mechanical, photocopying, recording or otherwise, without written permission from the copyright holder.

Thank you to so many family members and good friends who have participated in my "Boating Life" so far.
They may not be mentioned by name or shown in photographs but they know who they are. We look forward to many more adventures together.

A Boating Life
Adventures of a tiller girl

"What happens when my boat arrives on the lorry?" I asked the manager of the marina. "You drive it on to the mooring," he replied. "Not if you value the other boats," was my reply. "OK, Tom will do it for you."

After much research and starting my new job in Reading living in a motorhome, my new floating home had arrived from Thorne on a lorry. I knew I loved boats and the outdoors but narrowboats were a new direction for me, and for Diva, my crazy springer spaniel companion. Houses were more expensive in Reading than in Wales, my previous home, and I didn't want to take out a mortgage, only five years before retirement. I wanted to be able to support my mother, so I reasoned that I would just move the boat closer to her, whereas I would have to sell a house and buy another one. The option of living on a modern boat also seemed very exciting. I am sure that some friends and family members thought I was mad. However, looking back now, I am so glad I bought the boat. There have been some frightening moments but some fantastic ones too and sometimes you have to take a leap of faith, and hope.

Diva, my faithful boat companion for 10 years

My "floating home"

Friends and family were there to help on the arrival day and, once on the mooring, we thought the first phase was completed. However, I was about to be introduced to the vagaries of boat life, as I quickly discovered that the domestic water tank had been split in transit and would have to be removed for repair. A narrowboat has two main tanks, one wrapped around the stern for the fuel and one under the front deck for water. They balance one another. We also have a hot water tank under the bed. However, with the existing damage I was reduced to camping in my beautiful boat. Fortunately my new job was all consuming and, after a couple of weeks, the repair was completed. I was not deterred and set about learning to control my new vessel.

Outside working hours, fellow boaters were so helpful. This support is common in the whole boating community, as we normally work along the lines of what goes around comes around. I have made real friends over the years and am still in contact with folks I met as I "took to the water".

To return to my boat called *About Time*. It is a 50 foot /15.34 metres steel narrowboat with a cruiser stern. There are various types of stern on a narrowboat: the Trad, which, as it says, is what the original cargo carriers would have had. It is short so they could use as much of the boat as possible for cargo; then you have a semitrad, which has a short actual deck but an area in front of the stern deck where others can sit; finally, you have the cruiser stern, which is a larger area where you can gather and share the journey, which is the one I chose. The boat was built in 1997 by R & D and fitted out in 1998. I bought it in 2003. It is pine lined with central heating and a multifuel stove and now a cratch[1] and pram cover[1]. When it arrived it had single glazed windows, which have since been replaced by double glazed ones - so much better to avoid condensation and for noise reduction.

Every motorised boat needs the usual licence and four-yearly Boat Safety Certificate[2] plus insurance but, in addition, I have always paid for a subscription to RCR – River and Canal Rescue, like AA on the water. You can buy in on one of three levels: gold, silver or bronze at different prices. These offer greater or lesser rescue services according to your requirements. I, rightly or wrongly, concluded that if you have the boat engine serviced regularly and carry out maintenance, then the third level, bronze, is sufficient. This back up has proved very useful in smaller and larger ways, which I will explain later. I also joined the Residential Boat Owners' Association – RBOA. Boating matters can be frustratingly detached from land matters, possibly due to the fact that, in past decades, land and canals have developed side by side, but totally separately. The RBOA has been a very

Adventures of a tiller girl

informed and supporting group to belong to and I have also tried to do my bit with RBOA to publicise and promote things boating. Later on I was introduced to a second group, ironically called, the Tiller Girls. More and more single women were living on the "cut"[3] and this was, and is, a small but very supportive group whose members are naturally spread all over the country. I disqualified myself from the group after several years when we got married but that is another part of the story.

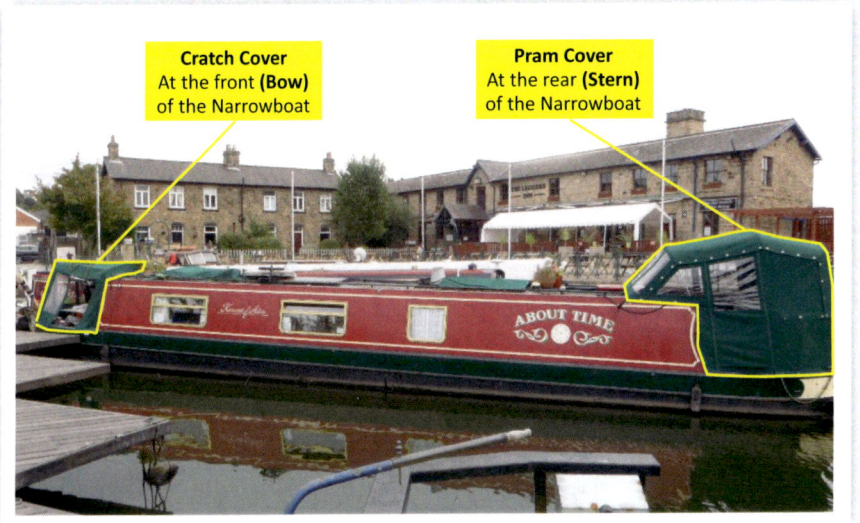

1   The front /bow cover on a narrowboat is called a cratch cover and, if it comes up and over, the stern cover is called a pram cover.
2   The Boat Safety Certificate, which takes place every four years, is like an MOT on a car but is not really concerned with the engine but more about fuel, gas and battery safety elements and appropriate ventilation.
3   The cut is a common name for the canal, originating from the waterway being cut through the countryside.

Learning to understand and move the boat

I was very keen to learn how to manage the vessel and coerced a fellow tutor, who taught on RYA[4] navigation courses, to give me a day's instruction. "I can't give you an Inland Waterways Certificate" he apologised. "Don't worry about that," I said, "I just want to learn to drive". In fact I got him to spend most of the day teaching me to go in and out of the mooring, so much so that the dog was sick! In addition, a few months later, Terry, from TR Holdings, came to give my daughter and myself a day's tuition to gain the Inland Waterways Helmsman Certificate. He, too, was a great help and taught us the basics on my boat. Some courses take place in a group and on someone else's boat. Boats are all different and handle differently so I think we got much more out of the day actually being on board *About Time*.

I used to laugh at myself because initially at the weekend I would take the boat from my mooring up the River Thames, turn in front of Caversham Lock and come back. I was too scared to go through the lock or to moor up to the bank on my own. Imagine my thrill, six months on, managing to travel up to Pangbourne and to stay overnight. All these years later, I can still remember my sense of achievement, even though the two locks I went through were manned by lockkeepers. I used to go through and say "Sorry, I have got L plates up" but the lockkeepers were so helpful, taking ropes and showing great patience.

At work, my colleagues were very supportive and were happy to share their past narrowboating experience, and, to join me on short or long trips. When I was still working full time you couldn't go too far as a narrowboat proceeds at a maximum of 4 miles an hour on canals and 6 miles an hour on rivers. Locks can take 20 minutes so that has to be factored in as well, not to mention going past moored boats on tick-over. You can never hurry life on the water and gradually I made sure that extra time was left for eventualities! I was taught a good lesson when my mother was coming on the bus to meet me in Devizes. In spite of doing 22 locks in one day with very energetic friends, I was still tight on time. The only way to get there was to leave at 5.30 am. Worried about disturbing other boaters moored at Honey Street, I pushed the boat away from the bank before starting the engine. The weather was kind to me and the scenery beautiful and I passed one of the white horses on the hill. I just managed to moor the boat and run to meet the bus, vowing again never to clock watch on boat trips. All visitors get warned that it's a lovely life but they cannot set an exact time schedule to it. Most love this element and find leaving time behind very acceptable. My son, Dan, was initially unimpressed by his mother's boat. He was a lorry driver and deemed the whole boating experience "so slow". Imagine my surprise when, six months after this pronouncement, he asked when he would be coming on board again. "But you said it was all far too slow for you," was my reply. "Ah yes", he said "but it is so relaxing."

Dan, my son, at the helm in Henley

Christina, my daughter at the helm in Reading centre

This photo of Chris comes with a health warning!

Young and old joined in - Carmen, my granddaughter, and Joshua, my grandson

My summer longer trips were always planned in February and sent in a computer document to family and friends. They would opt to join me on certain sections or meet me along the way. In the first eleven years of owning the boat I ended up doing about a third on my own and two thirds with friends and family. Thanks to everyone, we had some wonderful times on the boat. They even insisted later on that we met up on the system to celebrate my 60th, in 2008. I gradually gained in confidence, although it has to be said that my learning was occasionally by bitter experience or just ignorance.

My 60th birthday party - Gnosall on the Shropshire Union Canal

In hindsight my ignorance in early days was downright dangerous. "When was the last time you cleaned your chimney, Jane?" I had no idea. I had thought the fire wasn't pulling as well as before! Now the boat has 3 carbon monoxide sensors and a smoke alarm, I promoted the talk given by the Fire Service, and, I clean the chimney and baffle regularly. On another occasion I nearly flooded the engine, not to mention sinking the boat. I hadn't screwed down the greaser or advanced the bracket[5]. On About Time, and many other boats, you need to top up the grease around the propshaft regularly to stop water coming in. This should be obvious to even a beginner like me but it wasn't in my early boating days.

---

4   RYA – the Royal Yachting Association is an organisation that accredit many of the boating courses and qualifications

5   The propshaft has a stern gland packed with a type of rope and grease to prevent water from coming into the boat. The pressure is maintained by a bracket in the engine bay which needs to be tightened every so often. Finally there is often a brass greaser tube which you screw down at the end of every trip and this replaces any grease used.

Learning about marine mechanics

One situation kept frustrating me. My previous knowledge had been of petrol engines but now I had a marine diesel and whenever something went wrong the engineer would arrive and invariably give a sharp intake of breath. At that draw of breath, you knew that the price had just gone up ridiculously. In the early days some mechanics obviously thought here was a new ignorant boater and a woman to boot. I knew I had to do something to increase my own mechanical knowledge so I attended one of Tony Brooks' weekend engine courses at Reading College. "You can change the oil now", observed a fellow student. "Actually I am hoping never to have to do that," I replied "but I need to have enough knowhow to call the bluff of unscrupulous mechanics." Tony was a great tutor. I'm not sure I was such a good student but I had a little knowledge and it gave me some confidence to build on my understanding of the mechanics of my narrowboat.

Although I had wonderful friends who were very helpful in times of strife, I needed to find a reliable mechanic so I could be independent. I rang a local marine company with a good reputation to ask their advice and they recommended one of their employees, who now had a mobile service. Thank goodness! I rang Marcus and he took on the repair and servicing of the boat, continuing for several years. Patrick then took up the baton at Great Bedwyn.

Ray and Doreen, two of the friends who were so supportive.

Now to explore the waterways
(See map of canals and rivers on page 59)

There is something amazing about seeing the world from the water. Canals were there two hundred years ago and, since then, more roads and buildings have often been constructed around and over them. So much of the waterways is almost hidden from view. For example, I had never realised that there was a green corridor right into central London. You can only really see it from the river and the canals. Then there is the awe you feel as you enter Bristol Harbour, or Liverpool Dock or go under Clifton Bridge, with a pilot on board, which makes you feel like a real explorer. You think you have been to these places before but the thrill of entering them on the water gives you a whole new perspective. Leaving Honey Street early one morning I was accompanied by a pair of herons, one flying under the bridge and one flying over the top and that moment was the gift of a special oneness with nature. The beautiful scenery, spring flowers and even a horribly cold day, finished by mooring up and warming yourself by the fire, make you feel so secure and relaxed in your life on the water. However, I can still feel the shock when, on a dark still night, a fish jumped out of the water right beside me.

Bristol harbour viewed from the SS Great Britain

In the first few years, mainly in a longer summer break, I explored the Kennet and Avon Canal. What a contrast! Initially, you go through the centre of Reading, weaving in and out through the shops, sometimes on canal, sometimes on the

River Kennet itself. Then it's not long before you are out in the country, only to reach Aldermaston and that "feeling of power", as my brother called it, of holding up all the traffic by electrically lifting the bridge to allow boats to pass through. We did try to choose an appropriate moment to bring the cars to a standstill, honestly.

Daniel lifting the Aldermaston bridge

On the K & A, as it is lovingly called, the locks are large, some difficult and often very different, however, once across the beautiful open plain leading to Devizes, you reach the amazing Caen Hill Flight of 29 locks in total. We have taken the boat up and down the flight several times and each time we have formed a team of at least four people. I know boaters who have done it alone or with one other person – not my personal choice! It's also a great achievement and our team rounds off the day by a big meal which has been cooking on the last lap of the journey.

There are often CRT[6] volunteers to assist with locks and managing the boats passing one another. You usually arrive at the top or bottom of the flight the day before and try to pal up with another boat. Sometimes if the locks are to be set in your favour and you get a tip off from the lockkeepers to be in the lock for an early start, then you can really make good time.

A Boating Life

Caen Hill central 16 locks of 29

Approaching Caen Hill

From Caen Hill you are not far from the beautiful and historic towns of Bradford-on-Avon and Bath, reached by crossing two magnificent aqueducts.

You descend the locks into Bath and join the last part of the Canal's title,

Our team – from left to right – Elaine, Tony, myself, Alex and John the River Avon. There are several Avons in the United Kingdom and indeed the word *afon* is the word for *river* in Welsh. In times of good weather the descent from Bath to Bristol is easy and interesting as the river weaves through towns and meadows. You arrive at Netham Lock and have to stop to pay for your time in the Harbour. Bristol Harbour is an experience in itself. Waterside you can dine on the quay, enjoy the water ferries or visit the *SS Great Britain* and the *Matthew*. On the other hand you can go into the city to explore markets, history or culture. Apparently there are also caves under the city which we have yet to see.

There were many beautiful places on the way down the Avon

The Matthew in Bristol Harbour

The SS Great Britain

I have been up and down the 100 miles of the Kennet & Avon several times but its variety of moods and scenery never fail to please. There was one event which still makes my daughter laugh, although at the time we were not impressed. It was a fine day as we went through Newbury. I went up to help at the lock. Fortunately something made me look back at the boat only to see a foot disappear on to the back deck. This "delightful person" had obviously done this before and knew, once on the boat, he could go through the boat and our belongings and we would be totally occupied on the lock. I set off at a pace I didn't know I was capable of yelling "Get out of there you b.....d". The guy, hearing my yell, emerged from the boat. I grabbed his jacket but he got free and walked away. He knew I wouldn't leave the boat so he was able to disappear into the crowd. From then on our handbags were stored in the washing machine and the clip was on the back door before leaving the boat to go up to a lock. We tipped off any boat we passed to be careful on the Newbury Lock. Afterwards, Danusia, who was with me, was highly amused, as she had never seen me move so fast!

The canal life normally inspires a certain atmosphere of give and take. One day I was on my own on the canal, had the car nearby and had just been on a supermarket raid. I looked out and saw a man sitting in the stone cubby hole. He was evidently an itinerant. I was only too aware of the enormous pile of food I had just bought so went out to ask if I could offer him supper. Having given him supper wrapped in foil, I went to return to the boat at which point he stopped me. "I would like to recite a poem" he said and proceeded to relate one of his poems from his journey along the canal. It was a beautiful exchange.

In the early days, I made short journeys from the marina into the canal and each way along the River Thames. Gradually these got longer. I made it up to Oxford and on to the Oxford Canal. However, the fascination of going all the way to London on the river eventually became reality. It was amazing to feel that centuries of history had gone before you, particularly when, at that time, water was the safest way to travel.

No trip goes completely without its worrying moments. On the first of our trips to London, Henley was reached without a hitch, and likewise Marlow. The weather was pretty stormy and, although we were managing the strong currents, we didn't realise that they were putting up the red boards on the locks not long after we had gone through. Red boards mean inadvisable to travel. As we went through Cookham the current pulled the boat fiercely towards the bridge arches which meant you had to hold your nerve and fling the tiller over at the last moment. Joe and Jill were with me at that point and Joe's approach was "This is exciting, isn't it?" "No," I replied, "it's terrifying." Fortunately conditions calmed down and boating became less "exciting".

On another occasion I was going to London to meet my brother, John, and his wife, Anne, to go round the London Ring[7]. I reached Windsor and, mooring on the Eton bank, I had enjoyed exploring both sides of the river. Next day I was under way again in fine weather. I remember the planes from Heathrow were going overhead. The river wasn't busy and I was speaking to a friend on the mobile when a buzzing started. "Sounds like fan belt" Pam said. "Think you are right. Will have to ring off and check". That was all very well but the only place to moor was on the royal land of Windsor Castle. Every twenty yards was a sign saying no mooring and the equivalent of being thrown into the Tower if you were to do so! Offering my apologies to Ma'am, I rammed a stake into her lawn and tied the boat on. Surprise! Surprise! The estate manager arrived within minutes and announced the arrival of security police bearing guns. Needless to say I quickly offered ID. "How long before you can leave?" they asked. "As short a time as possible "I replied, "if you give RCR clearance through your gate. They are on the way" Fortunately, the fan belt was quickly replaced, I thanked them and left. It wasn't until I got to Teddington and was laughingly relating my adventure to the lockkeeper that I heard the whole truth. Terrorists had been threatening to hijack a narrowboat, fill it with explosives, and then detonate it in front of the Houses of Parliament. Sure enough on our way back, with Roger Squires as our pilot and passing Westminster, a police patrol boat drew up alongside us and asked for ID. I was able to say that they already had my ID. They laughed and were very pleased with some of Annie's cakes passed from one boat to the other.

My brother John and his wife Anne in front of the Houses of Parliament

Glad to offer sustenance to the long-suffering police

John Maxfield and his partner, Annie Topham, the cake maker!, on the "up the Thames" trip

Fortunately, on all trips, I have kept a log. My family and friends are always asking one another when we were in such and such a place, so the logs answer these questions and make great reading. They don't tell you useful things, for some, like how much diesel we used but reminds us of where we moored, any event and who we met – names of people and boats. This latter fact has proved very useful. Some boaters have amazing memories and, on meeting you again after three or four years will call out "Hi Jane how are you?"(May be once seen never forgotten!) Now I might be able to recall many of the details of our conversations but names are not my strong point, so it's back to the log to save face.

---

6   CRT stands for Canal & River Trust. This organisation replaced British Waterways. CRT is now a charity and has a much wider profile involving many sections of society. It is responsible for the waterways' maintenance but also promotes the canals and rivers as a place to relax and exercise and has many volunteers.

7   The London Ring can be taken clockwise or anticlockwise. We started at Teddington, went off the River into Brentford and turned right into the Regents Canal. We went through London Zoo and Camden Market, Victoria Park and into Limehouse Basin. From there we took on a pilot and came up the Thames past St Pauls, Westminster, under so many famous bridges and up to Teddington.

Moving to Great Bedwyn

I had had a wonderful time at Reading, thanks to so many friends and colleagues, however, I knew that, when I retired in 2008, I wanted to be nearer my mother in Fordingbridge. So I put my name down for a canal mooring with CRT and fortunately, in 2007, one came up in Great Bedwyn, a beautiful Wiltshire village. This was probably the closest I could get to Mum on the canal, so I accepted readily. It did mean several months of longer journeys to work but was a chance not to be missed.

My next learning curve in boating began. There was no electricity on the mooring and, in addition, the mooring was on the offside[8]. This meant a walk round from the car park with any shopping. Obviously, this walk was highly welcomed by a certain furry friend and, from the time of our arrival, she delighted in a long stretch of bank where she could wander not causing any problem to herself or the other boaters.

Back to the boat and the changes necessary to live well without a mains electric feed for the boat. On my bank mooring I would have to use the engine or a generator to recharge the batteries but had identified several things I could alter to improve my standard of living. Solar panels were relatively new on a boat in 2007, which, writing in 2020, seems amazing. Alternative energy has come such a long way since then. I had two 90 watt panels fitted to the boat and a control panel for £1000, thinking that they would pay for themselves, against the cost of fuel, in five years. Actually, as it happened, the cost of diesel went through the roof and they paid for themselves in three years. We only replaced them for two 165 watt panels in 2019 and so we had free solar electricity for 9 years! Incidentally, the cost of the replacement was about the same all those years later and we now have panels providing nearly twice the power.

The second major alteration was installing the wind turbine, mounted on the boat. It wasn't the easiest of gadgets because it had to be stored in the summer, when we were off on trips, and to hoist it on its pole needed two or three people but it was a useful addition to the power source. Marcus wanted to try fitting them on boats so he said if I bought the kit he would fit it for free. We didn't add this to the boat until I had arrived in Great Bedwyn and were very pleased with ourselves once achieved. It must be said, and much to local amusement, we didn't have a breath of wind for the first five weeks after installation.

Another major change, apart from replacing lights with LEDs, was installing a 12volt fridge instead of the 240volt one. This would mean that I didn't have to run the inverter[9] and could save more power.

All these amendments really did make a difference and lessen the worry of coming in after work to low batteries. I couldn't run the engine late at night as that would disturb fellow boaters or village residents. The carrying of heavy shopping etc around from the car was solved by a big trolley, a lovely surprise from a good friend, and I could also use the dinghy to go across to the car park on the opposite side. The dog loved coming in the little boat and I found rowing so relaxing so we used it whenever we could. The dinghy also had another amazing use. In the winter of 2010 the canal froze over for several weeks. We tied a rope to both sides of the canal and the dinghy became a toboggan. It dutifully transported everything, including coal and water, across the canal until the ice thawed and we were able to move our boats some five weeks later.

The snow arrived in 2010

Adventures of a tiller girl

*2010 and the freeze – Chris swimming on thick ice!
The rope across the ice to the dinghy*

Whilst in Bedwyn I looked at the interior of the boat and decided on new curtains. Annie duly created beautiful ones, and a new bedsettee. I wanted to preserve comfortable seating at the same time as comfortable sleeping. We just managed a 6 foot settee which expanded into a 4'6" bed. Alex has had to amend the slats but the couch is still in very good condition a decade later. Worth paying the money to have one made to measure.

My new curtains and bed settee

---

8   The offside of a canal is the oppositeside to the towpath.

9   The inverter on "About Time" is a combi unit which provides 240v electricity. When connected to electricity in the marina it also charges the batteries and allows us to have a standard 240v supply. When out on the water it converts the battery power to 240volts for television and washing machine whilst lights, pumps and fridge stay on 12volt

Boat life in Bedwyn

My stay in Great Bedwyn was very special. Yes, being there got me much closer to my mother but it was also a brilliant place to live. Positioned just south of Marlborough and with its own railway station, it was perfectly positioned for contact with the outside world whilst also being completely self contained. We had a post office – happy to provide a poste restante address; a doctor's surgery – happy to take boaters on as patients, not always so easy; a general store, a baker's, a church, a hairdresser's and two pubs. There was also a thriving choir, which I joined, and various other sports and social clubs. From the moorings you could go on a lovely circular walk incorporating the shops or you could escape into the woods and fields.

When I moved to Bedwyn my friends and colleagues said I had to have a housewarming party so we had a mooring party. Fortunately the weather was amazing and we sat out in the sun while a friend's grandchildren rowed around in the dinghy with a long rope on it. Although I provided a lot of the food, everyone brought something and we dined royally. Obviously, there was one slight problem and that was once the Elsan/ chemical toilet cassettes became full so yet again the dinghy came in handy to take said items to the services on the other side.

Much hilarity as Debbie and Barry take the Elsan across

Another special Bedwyn element was the Bruce Trust. David and Louise Bruce had established the trust by buying the first boat equipped for holidays for disabled people. They went on to establish a fleet of boats, specifically adapted for families or friends, accompanying disabled children or adults, to go on holiday on the canal. Later there was also a large motorhome. The trust had a permanent engineer, an administrator and several trainers but the rest of the work – cleaning and painting – was done by volunteers, in fact a team of over 100.

Not a housewarming but a mooring party

We used to opt into a rota so you could help as often or as little as you wanted to. It was a marvellous gang which produced wonderful experiences for the groups and families. The Bruce Trust even had a boat at the Paralympics in London 2012.

Diana, one of the Bruce Trust boats, before travelling down the K & A and the Thames to the Olympic Park

My mother sadly had to move into a residential home in 2009 but, on one occasion, we hired one of the boats for herself and some of her friends. It was so lovely for them all to be out in nature and where their lack of mobility was not a problem. After several decades of hard work and fund raising David and Louise have now retired but the boats have been taken over by the Kennet & Avon Canal Trust.

On board Hannah, adapted for disabled boaters

For steam enthusiasts, Great Bedwyn is only a couple of miles from Crofton Pumping Station. They run very popular gala days and we would always hear or see the various steam machines on their slow way to Crofton. Not being a steam enthusiast in the know, I didn't realise Crofton's fame until one day, while on the wharf, I got talking to some Australians who had brought their hire boat through Bedwyn. I think I asked them why they had chosen to hire on the K & A. but was not expecting the reply that they had come to see the engine at Crofton. Apparently there was a sister engine in a small

Gala day at Crofton

The Crofton Pumping Station

town in New South Wales on the other side of the world. Often the boats would congregate for the Crofton rallies and, through these gatherings, I joined Pewsey Wharf Boat Club, one of the small cruising clubs around the system. Cruising clubs are privately run. They have varying numbers of members and facilities but often have a long history.

There was always something to do on the boat and every spring I would work around the boat, sanding down the rust and painting the hull. The dinghy was a very useful tool, allowing me to go all the way round. It was hard work but the sounds of the village, the trains and the canal plus the birds made it a very relaxing activity.

Water balances Life

The music plays,
The sound is carried over the water.
The dinghy tours the hull,
Helping with painting
And the breeze blows over the canal,
Over the water.

Gentle sounds reach the ears -
Boats loading, people talking,
Cars on the bridge,
A train passing -
And the sounds drift over the canal,
Over the water.

The day, tho' closing,
Feels contented, unthreatening.
Life is not rushing,
No urgent mobile rings.
For an instant there are no demands,
And the breeze blows over the canal,
Over the water.

Staying on the bank mooring at Great Bedwyn was actually much more physical than being in the marina but, on the other hand, I was more involved in canal matters and often waved or chatted to passing boaters. Friends even chose Bedwyn for a winter mooring[10]. So a chance to catch up.

Every year, in April, we all cleared the main channel and watched while the young and not so young competitors in the Devizes to Westminster canoe race went through. They have various practice stages earlier in the year but the actual race takes place over 24 hours, the present record standing at under 16 hours. Originally started in 1951 and with the canal in disrepair, it took around 90 hours to complete. Various classes have been introduced over the years and now there are junior competitors. They are not allowed to carry on through the night so there are three official resting points at which they must overnight.

In my time at Bedwyn the K & A celebrated its 200th Anniversary in 2010. There were many events up and down the canal but we had an appropriate wharf party with dignitaries and boats suitably decorated. Over the early 20th century the canal had fallen into disrepair, with the competition from both road and rail, but, after incredible efforts from the volunteers to complete the restoration, the Queen had reopened the K and A in 1990. Once more you could travel all the way from London to Bristol on the Thames and the canal.

Two of the competitors in the annual Devizes to Westminster Race

In order to address the needs of all its residents, Wiltshire was instructed, as were all councils at the time, to produce a report about the minority groups in the area. These included travellers, migrant workers, Army wives, boaters, disabled people and others.

Celebration of 200 years of the Kennet and Avon Canal

All decorated for the K&A 200th Anniversary event

Wiltshire decided not to create a hardcopy report which could be left to gather dust but to make a short film about each group. When it came to boaters, we had several meetings to ascertain the elements to be reported and then filming began. It was a very well balanced summary of life on the water in Wiltshire, the advantages and disadvantages. It featured many conversations with boaters from all walks of life and discussed problems and solutions. The dog and I were filmed at Bedwyn and I was proud to be part of it. The films were then uploaded on to the Wiltshire website.

I shall always remember the years at Bedwyn. In 2009 I stopped part time teaching and spent several years going back and forth to be with Mum in the home. Two years later we had to sell her house in Fordingbridge to fund her care. At that point I had to decide exactly what I wanted or could bring on the boat. I had always said I would not "store" any belongings. Obviously one or two items of family value stayed with cousins but I had to be very selective. I saved all the photos and had them copied on to CDs. That was a big job but all family members have copies so we haven't lost any of those memories.

About Time actually played a part at the end of our family's sixty years' life in Fordingbridge. The local secondary school was running an auction of promises to raise some much needed funds. Having consulted the insurers, I offered a day on the boat for a family. The school was delighted and the family, who bought the day trip, was charming and great fun. They eventually wanted to hire a boat and this was their introduction to the canals. Over the years there have been three day trips on the boat "bought at charity auctions".

Sadly, Mum died in June 2012, at the wonderful age of 97. In order to think through future plans, I stayed in Caen Hill Marina, near Devizes, over the winter and realised that I could now plan the big trip up north I had thought about but couldn't entertain before.

I had dreamt about going up through Standedge Tunnel on the Huddersfield Canal, over to Liverpool and crossing the Mersey with a pilot. Various friends had expressed interest in different stages. Alex, whom I had met in 2012, said he would join me in September in Yorkshire as he loved that area.

Mum loved the life outdoors

I made my preparations, sold the wind turbine and the generator and gave up my Bedwyn mooring. I set off for my "big trip" in May 2013.

---

10 Boaters who do not have a regular mooring and are "continuous cruisers" can, if they wish, pay for a winter mooring. Certain places will be designated by CRT and you can apply to take one of these moorings.

You win a few and lose a few

You consciously try to pay water, and its possible dangers, great respect but sometimes situations arise which emphasize the need to be always on your guard. Two such events happened when I was in Great Bedwyn.

It was a fine day and an engineer was replacing the batteries on *About Time* on the wharf. Another narrowboat passed through and at the same moment a young girl without a life jacket fell off the trad stern. Mother, of diminutive stature, panicked and jumped in still wearing her boots. We now had two people floundering in the canal. The engineer and I automatically started to take off our shoes and jump in when a much smaller narrowboat, the crew having seen the problem, nipped out round my boat and plucked both from the water. All was well but it could have been so different.

The other occasion took place on a cold October evening. A family of older Mum and Dad, one daughter and her husband and a second disabled daughter had moored their hire boat in Bedwyn overnight. The husband had just left to secure a table at the pub nearby. I was on the wharf too when suddenly I heard "Help! Help!". Initially I thought it was teenagers larking about but then realised the cries were serious. I went out quickly and discovered, to my horror, that the elderly father had walked his disabled daughter off the wrong side of the boat. The able bodied sister was trying desperately to save them. We had a rope on the boat roof with a loop tied into the end and I threw it to her, saying "tell them to put a foot in it and let me know when to pull". We had the freezing twosome out of the water on to the deck in no time. The husband was recalled from the pub and I felt so sorry for him as his guilt at not being there to help was obvious but completely unfounded. I rinsed and dried some of their clothes round my fire while they all went up to the pub for supper, none the worse for their exploits, but all of us aware of how quickly things can change for the worse.

Unfortunately, however much research you do and preparation you make, things don't always go according to plan. That's how it turned out in 2013. The big trip, as I called it, went really well for the first few months. I met friends, explored new waterways and even did the 12 Bosley Locks singlehanded.

Elaine met me in Stalybridge on the Huddersfield Canal. She had recently lost her father and I had suggested she join me and have a bit of a break. We had a lovely restful first evening and enjoyed her homemade Lasagne. Off we set the next morning, going through a few locks and stopping to fill up with water.

We got to 9W on the Huddersfield and took the boat in. Elaine was locking, the boat rose up and the top gate opened. The boat went so far through and the bow stuck on the top of the lock. I tried to reverse but it wouldn't go forward or backwards. What I also hadn't realised was that the water was escaping out of the bottom gates quite quickly and so, with the bow stuck on the top cill of the lock, the back of the boat dropped, taking water into the engine bay. Thank goodness there was no one else on the boat and the dog was on the lock with Elaine. The engine gurgled and I rushed to turn it off, grabbed my mobile from the back cubbyhole and leapt for the lock wall. Once on the lock, and with the water level in the lock going down, I grabbed centre and bow ropes and tied them on to every piece of lock machinery around the top gate.

CRT employees were on the scene amazingly quickly, considering the isolated position of lock 9W. They drained the pound[11] below the lock which, in turn, drained Lock 9W and actually helped the inside of the boat. Even though the back half, with all the contents, had been underwater, this was drained out after an hour and a half. The boat was now at a rakish angle. RCR arrived and we were forbidden from going on to collect any of our possessions. The boat was only held by its own ropes and so it was arranged that there would be watch on the boat overnight and RCR would attempt to refloat her the following day.

We were now the problem for RCR as Elaine and I had only what we were standing up in plus my mobile, no money, no dog lead nor dog food. A hotel

The boat stuck on the top cill of the lock

Being refloated from this disaster

which would take the dog was found and David Omeroyd, the engineer, said he'd drop us off. He even offered to get some cash for us which we refused but were so touched as he had never met us. Since we have moved up north permanently, David has become our boat engineer but that is another part of the story.

We arrived at Grains Bar Hotel in Oldham and again Pat and her husband were so helpful, producing the best tasting tinned soup and ham sandwiches ever! Their kitchen was closed. They had dogs and fed Diva with their dog food. My mobile was fast running out of charge and they also produced a box of chargers, left behind by various guests. Once I had found a matching one, it was "just keep it" Phew! I rang my daughter and she transferred money to the hotel so that we could pay and have some cash for essentials!

That night the dog slept on the bath mat and we have often remembered the ironical comment I made as we prepared for sleep, "Well we won't need to worry about what to wear tomorrow" Poor Elaine she had been with me for 36 hours. So much for her having a relaxing holiday! Once again we were overwhelmed by the kindness. The following morning another hotel guest insisted on driving us to the local shop to buy essentials like toothpaste and toothbrushes. The same guest drove us all the way back to the canal.

When we arrived back at the boat, RCR were already there and they had used enormously thick ropes to tie on to trees above the lock and take the strain of the boat's own ropes. Miraculously the ropes had held but the RCR engineer needed to tell me that if the boat slipped off the top of the lock in the refloating process the boat would break her back.

A crowd had formed and we all watched from the safety of a nearby bridge and I held my breath! They wrapped plastic around the stern of the boat, installed pumps and let water into the lock. Gradually the boat came to the normal position and was floating! We offloaded as many of the wet belongings as we could. Guy came up from his marina at Portland Basin to tow her back to his marina. He had to tow the boat on up the canal to turn round and then tow her back.

We had finally retrieved our handbags and Elaine's car key. Would the keyfob still work after its dunking? She went to fetch the car and amazingly the key worked. Some time during the process we met up with Lee who also kindly helped us offload more possessions before Guy came to take the boat the rest of the way. We found a wonderful laundrette and Keren, the proprietress, took the mountains of wet clothes and bedding. She was amazed at how much you could get on a narrowboat. We were thrilled when we collected the first dry load as we, at last, had some clean clothes! We moved hotel to be nearer the boat and continued to retrieve the wet items. It actually took several weeks to remove, photograph and deal with the wet contents.

The insurers, Haven Knox Johnson, were so helpful from day one but pointed out initially that I was only covered for a few days in a hotel. Anyway, Elaine needed to get back home and I needed to collect my car so we combined her journey south with a two day stopover at Stafford to stay with friends and a bit of relaxation for the first time since the accident.

While I was away Lee had put up his large tent for me in a nearby campsite and that was to be my home for the next month. I was so grateful to have somewhere to stay on my return. Actually the site was at Greenfield and had a wonderful backdrop of hills and woods. It was a perfect place to retreat to after many a day working on the boat. The dog was very happy too, although I had to dissuade her from chasing sheep. She hadn't met sheep before!

My view from the tent, the hills above Uppermill

Once again so many people came to help and support me. Christina, my daughter, arrived on my second day at the campsite. It was lovely to see her. She is very practical and asked what I wanted her to do. "Move the tent to a flatter part of the site, please" It was moved. She pitched her tent beside mine and I started to feel there might be life after the accident.

So many family members and friends, new and old, were amazing and either travelled to keep me company or actually work on the boat with me. The whole of the back half of the boat had been underwater and gradually the wet and damaged possessions and machinery were taken off. Obviously those items that had escaped the dunking in the Huddersfield also had to come off. The insurers sent Anthony up from Southampton to help with the process. It is one thing to look after your boat, on a normal basis, but I had no idea, after the accident, what to do first or what needed to be replaced or ordered. Anthony pointed out to myself and Guy what needed to be removed. He took me to Currys with my laptop and instigated a report on the damage. We gathered up packing boxes in which to store new or clean items in the newly rented self storage unit.

Every day I donned my expensive overalls – large black litter sacks! –over my jeans and offloaded more muddy items. All the wet documents were hung out on the fences at the campsite with pegs. Every damaged item was photographed for the insurers. The marina pumped out the engine, replaced the oil and it started. I'd saved it by switching it off so quickly. The engine loom and the inverter were replaced and so it went on. The dehumidifiers were going night and day. The new floor coverings went down, the new fridge went in and the boat was industrially cleaned.

We were making progress but I need to return to the accident for a moment. There had been a similar situation at the same lock two years previously. Local people told me about it and so I started to investigate. The other boat had been going down whereas we had been going up. They had caught on the top of lock 9W too. I realised that these accidents could have been avoided if there had been minimum depth posts installed. I spoke to the owner of the other boat, a respected marina owner. I approached the manager of the North West CRT and he tried to blame the other skipper when talking to me and blame me when talking to others. I was determined this wouldn't happen to someone else, plus the fact that had there been a small child or older person on board with me I may not have been able to save them. I was promised these posts for October. However, following several further phone calls, they were finally installed six months later. Management at CRT only heard about this whole problem some eighteen months later, through an article I wrote for RBOA's *Soundings*. I had written about the whole year, its ups and downs. I had said how sad it was that boaters and management couldn't work together. The manager wrote an apology then and, fortunately, even in these few intervening years, life on the waterways has become more mutually supportive.

Back to the restoration of the boat. Even though many of the jobs had been done on the boat, Portland Basin wasn't a big marina and they had hire boats to look after. The work on *About Time* was taking up considerable time and effort. Once we had got to a certain point Haven Knox Johnson agreed to me taking the boat to the bigger Swanley Bridge Marina to finish the project.

---

11 The pound is the water between two locks. Sometimes it can be several miles long and sometimes, as in this case, it was about 150 yards/50yds.

The dog and I were joined by a special person

Actually, as it turned out, I was to have a companion for this next journey. In 2012, whilst on holiday in Germany, I had met up with Alex and we had talked boats. He explained that he had sadly had to give up his cruiser two years previously. I, in turn, told him how lots of family and friends joined me on boat trips at different stages so, once the plan for 2013 trip had been prepared, I had sent it to Alex and he opted to join me in early September in Yorkshire. Following the accident, plans had obviously changed and I suggested that he either came in the spring of 2014, when the boat would be back on the water, or he could take a room in a hotel near the campsite for a few days and we could explore the area. I needed to have a break as I had been working on the boat continuously for a month. He decided to book in locally so we spent the next few days wandering the canals and hills in the beautiful area around Marsden and Uppermill. It wasn't until the end of his stay that we realised that a chance meeting on a walking holiday and our shared love of boats had greater implications than either of us could ever have imagined. A week or so later we agreed he would help me move the boat to Swanley Bridge in October. A new chapter in both our lives was about to start.

Before leaving Portland Basin, I really wanted to thank my new local friends for all their help and support. There was Lee, who had helped from the beginning; Chris, who had a caravan on the campsite and kept my spirits up with her great sense of humour; Kay who had befriended me one evening in the pub and continued to be so supportive; and Keren, who had taken all our soggy belongings into the laundrette, with her charming son, Edward. They are all still friends. So I invited them to have a day out on the boat.

The day was fine and we had great fun. Having lunched we turned round. All had gone very well until we got within a few miles of the marina and went through a bridge hole. The boat stopped suddenly. Try as we may, it would not go backwards or forward. Lee got into the water and we discovered we were stuck on a supermarket trolley! I couldn't believe it. This was my first day out on the boat after the accident. My friends had to walk to the nearest road where they could get a taxi back to their cars and I stayed on board, blocking the canal, until Guy could come out early the next morning and rescue the boat for the second time in two months! Actually he had a major problem pulling the boat off the trolley. Thank goodness that after half an hour or so the boat was again under her own power and no longer an obstacle to other canal users.

Moving on

The accident had been on 4th August and it was now October. If we were going to move the boat it had to be soon. Alex and I had arranged to meet in Castlefield and he would join me there for the journey to Swanley Bridge. Before arriving at Castlefield there were the 18 locks of the Ashton Canal plus the Rochdale 9. Christina said she'd come up and help and Mark, from the next door boat, and his nephew, Stuart, kindly volunteered to help with the first 18. Then Bruce joined me to do the Rochdale 9 through Manchester. All four of them really helped to restore some of my confidence. Once again I was extremely grateful to family and friends.

Bruce and I moored the boat and had a beer to celebrate completing the Rochdale 9. The locks are fascinating and some could call them daunting. The top one is actually under a building and you drive into the dark amongst the pillars supporting the building above. Later you are alongside busy roads and cafes and restaurants on the canalside and finally you pass to the rear of the Bridgewater Hall. Our last of the nine locks emptied into the waterside area of Castlefield, with its clubs and bars, and situated at the eastern end of the Bridgewater Canal.

Through Manchester on the Rochdale 9

Alex arrived a couple of days later. We went to the late night at the Manchester Art Gallery and then dined at a Turkish restaurant, the *Topkapi Palace,* which Alex had visited 40 years earlier! The following day we couldn't leave for Swanley until the new washing machine had arrived. It came, as arranged, on the dockside, so to speak.

We were now ready to go. We cast off, travelling on the Bridgewater Canal to work our way south.

The Bridgewater Canal was the first canal in the UK to be built and runs from Leigh and Worsley to Runcorn with an arm going into Manchester. It was built without locks – an amazing feat of engineering! Leaving Manchester, there was plenty to see. We went past Trafford Park and caught sight of the Manchester Ship Canal. Had we turned north we would have come to the amazing Barton Aqueduct which actually crosses the Ship Canal.

More of the Rochdale 9

However, this time we turned south and the journey took us through Sale and Lymm. We didn't rush so were able to explore these very different little towns on the way.

We turned on to the Trent & Mersey Canal and through the 1239 yards of Preston Brook Tunnel. Not long after that we stopped at Dutton Breach, whose name originated from the event in 2012 when hundreds of tons of water, earth and stone literally poured down from the canal into the farmer's fields below. Following a £2.1 million repair, some lovely moorings, overlooking

Bottom lock empties into Castlefield. No water shortage!

the Weaver valley, were created. You are several miles from shops, and modern civilisation, but you have the views, the woods and the farm sounds around you. Whenever we go that way we try to allow ourselves to stop for a couple of days to enjoy the tranquillity.

Nature calms and enlivens the soul - from Dutton Breach

The early morning trains trundled across the viaduct,

Hiding momentarily behind the woods,

And, for those seconds, barely audible.

For decades the scene has altered little,

As ever the cows graze in the lush fields,

In pastures, which were that day

Sodden from the recent storms.

Several houses, not new, are caught up

In the vast panorama.

The river's weir construction rises, almost inobtrusively,

In a corner of this wonderful landscape.

You hold your breath, nervously,

As though the picture before you might disappear.

At each special visit, on reaching the hedge,

You are forced to stop, to add other details,

To record more of this image-

The sharpness of colour and shade,

Or the gentle caress of the breeze,

Willing your memory not to forget

And to easily recall the wonder and awe

Of this serenity and beauty,

Repainting this picture vividly in our minds

So that one day soon, like an invisible thread,

It will draw us back.

May 2019

The Anderton Lift

We reluctantly left Dutton and journeyed on to Anderton. We have since taken the boat down on the exciting Anderton lift but on this occasion we went down to the Weaver and back up as foot passengers and enjoyed the detailed commentary.

Alex had originally said he would stay on board with me for six days but actually came all the way to Swanley. We turned up the Middlewich Branch and then into the Hurleston Locks at the entrance to the Llangollen Canal. Just a short while after the flight of locks, we arrived at Swanley Bridge Marina. We would stay there until the following summer while further repairs took place; while the boat was repainted. This booking had already been made the previous year; and, finally, we had to wait for a tricky operation for Alex in the May.

A Boating Life

Cruising together

It's amazing how life moves on. Our chance meeting on a walking holiday led us both to having new life partners with all the caring and sharing, joy and health problems that brings with it.

On the boat, obviously, there was the beauty of exploring the waterways together but, in addition to this, Alex had years of boating experience and also a training in engineering (very useful in many repairs!). He gently and wonderfully supported my ragged nerves to regain confidence after the nightmare of the accident. However, he personally had always been involved with cruisers and yachts. A 50 foot steel narrow boat, with a diesel engine at one end, a flat bottom and two thirds of the boat above the waterline, was not, therefore, his favourite marine vessel. A few years, on Alex has well and truly mastered the movements of this ungainly boat.

The dog was less than enthusiastic about Alex' arrival. She was now eleven years old. On deck she would lean against him by way of pushing him off the boat. He, in turn, was very caring towards her but that didn't change her approach. Diva was also beginning to show her eleven years. She was going deaf and was partially sighted. We had to watch her carefully because

A few years on, a relaxed Alex at the helm

she fell off the bank into the water several times, misjudging how far away the water was. She had previously always been biddable about staying put on the boat until it was safe and never jumped in off the bank, only going in for a swim when the bank sloped gently into the canal or stream. Travelling backwards and forwards from house to boat now was difficult for her, whereas for years she had loved the boat life. We had her company until the end of 2015 when she suffered mini strokes. Her ashes have been scattered in the wonderful pet cemetery in the hills above Rossendale, where her commemorative plaque reads: "Diva, much loved, free to chase rabbits again."

Over the years since Alex and I got together, he has had various trips to hospital fighting bowel and liver cancer and has bravely overcome the problems that go with this major surgery. There is fortunately sometimes a funny side to these traumatic events. In June 2014, after the first of these operations, we were back on the boat on the Coventry Canal. Alex asked me to marry him early one morning and I very happily accepted. However, by the end of that momentous day Alex was having medical problems and we needed to ring his original hospital and then a local ambulance. "Where are you?" they asked. "I'm not sure" I replied. "What is the bridge number?" Impressive, I gave them the number and, by the time we were walking down the towpath, the paramedic was walking towards us with all the equipment. He took us to the hospital and Alex was admitted.

The only problem was, emerging into the sunshine at 6am the following morning, I had no idea where I was. I managed to get a taxi driver to take me back to the boat but it was a very expensive trip. So I looked at the map and worked out that I could take the boat to within a ten minute walk of the George Eliot Hospital at Nuneaton where Alex was being treated. The slow boat journey time would mean I would be late visiting Alex. I rang the ward sister and asked if she could give Alex a message, telling her she would probably not understand it but he would. She went to Alex and said bemusedly, "Your wife rang and the message is that she won't be in for a while because she is moving the boat closer".

Over the years we made several trips to A & E in various hospitals, so much so that we laughingly dubbed him "the NHS' secret shopper" and, as we set off on a new trip I reminded him ironically that he had no need to continue in his secret shopper role. One instance, which actually wasn't based on an existing condition, involved a trip to Wrexham hospital.

Having arranged to leave the boat at Crick Marina, we were very slowly reversing into a berth. I paused the boat for Alex to get off with the centre line and continued with the manoeuvre. Seconds later I turned back to see Alex propelled into the air and into the water, catching his back on the boat. The jetty was far from stable and had acted like a trampoline. I managed to pull the boat away from him and we helped him, in pain, up the ladder. Once he had showered and dressed we drove to Wrexham A & E. Two hours later we were with the doctor who had X-rayed his back. "You have broken a rib but don't worry you have eleven others. Just take your usual painkillers and it will get better" We haven't got any "usual painkillers" we explained and were given paracetamol. Alex insisted on carrying on with life as usual and the operation, scheduled for the next week, was given the green light by his own consultant!

A Boating Life

Even the wedding involved the boat

Our first planned boat trips together were centred around our wedding and moving house. We needed to choose a good place for friends and family to come to join our wedding party and somewhere on or near a canal. We decided on Aylesbury and we were able to base the boat temporarily at the Aylesbury Canal Society basin. For our special weekend we moored the boat outside the Travelodge and were married on Friday September 19th 2014 at the Gateway Aylesbury.

It was all a bit touch and go because Alex was post operative and only just managed to recover in time to be able to enjoy the weekend. His relatives from Scotland were the first to arrive on the Thursday and the last of our friends and family left on the Sunday. We had a marvellous time. The service was beautiful and we followed it by a buffet and disco with our 50 guests in a local hostelry. The following day, and thanks to several friends, we had another buffet, but this time, at the boat on the canal side. We thought that there would be about 20 people but actually 35 friends and family carried on the party.

Following the wonderful wedding weekend, we returned in the boat to the Aylesbury Canal Society basin to a fabulous welcome and even a banner. We shared wedding food and drink and had a dance around the club kitchen! What a special time!

The canal side picnic outside the Travelodge

Before we met, Alex owned a house, which he was sharing with two of his sons. Previous to our meeting, he had talked about selling up. A month before the wedding a buyer came along. Neil and Andrew started looking for a house near Neil's work in Stevenage. Loving Yorkshire and Lancashire, Alex and I knew we wanted to find a house to the east of Manchester, near the moors and near the canals. However, we hadn't had a honeymoon so at the end of September, we sorted out the boat and headed north.

Looking for a guest house we could stay at on our way up to Scotland, we had found the beautiful self catering Squirrel Cottage, in Denshaw, overlooking the moors. We spent three days enjoying the moors and hills and looking at houses. Finally, we decided to leave for Scotland. We had one more house to view. We walked into it, liked it, discussed it, whilst sat in the car, and agreed a price with the vendors! It was meant to be. Completely coincidentally, Squirrel Cottage, Grains Bar Hotel, where Elaine and I had stayed the night after the accident, and our new street were all on the Ripponden Road.

We continued on up to Scotland, seeing relatives, exploring Alex' old haunts and, inevitably going to boat oriented attractions, like the Falkirk Wheel and the Crinan Canal. It was a fabulous ten days but we knew that we had to return to sorting out Alex' house at Letchworth. Thank goodness we had the boat moored not far away at Aylesbury so we could escape the packing and trips to the charity shop and also give the guys a bit of peace! The first sale fell through but another buyer was found. After much searching, Neil and Andrew found an appropriate house near Neil's work. The moving date was set for early January 2015. We all worked very hard and they moved in. Our house up north would not be ready until February so Alex' possessions went into store and we lived on the boat for a month. With help from Dan, Chris and Rebecca we finally moved into our little house in Oldham and we would, over the next few years, gradually move the boat nearer to the house in a round about way!

The year became half on board half at the house

We spend as much of the year as we can in the boat, doing house projects in the winter. With the odd week on shore for family events, we are normally on board from March to September/ October and then the occasional cruise in the winter. In 2015, following our house move, we went round the London ring, my second time, and we extended that trip by going up the Lea Navigation, past the Queen's Jubilee Barge at the Olympic Park.

The Queen's jubilee barge at the Olympic Park

Sadly we couldn't go around the park itself as the waterway was still under construction but we travelled on up to Hertford seeing the beautiful gazebos at Ware. The Lea Navigation is an amazing green corridor running down the east side of Greater London.

Gazebos at Ware

Once back in London we paused in Limehouse Basin before going out on to the tidal Thames. Again Roger Squires kindly volunteered to pilot the boat. It was my second time up from Limehouse to Teddington but that trip never ceases to thrill.

We travelled on up the Thames to Reading and turned on to the Kennet & Avon Canal,

Chris, Alex and myself on the way up the tidal part of the Thames to Teddington

wintering that year in Newbury. Newbury was an excellent base to further explore Berkshire. When spring arrived we went on down to Bath and Bristol Harbour and, very early one July morning, with a Bristol pilot, Alex' two sons and John on board, we travelled under Clifton Bridge, down to Avonmouth, to Portishead Marina and up the Severn Estuary in beautiful sunshine.

Andrew, Alex' son, on board for the Severn Estuary Trip

We were all elated on arriving at Sharpness but exhausted. Due to freak weather conditions we had had to leave Cumberland Basin at 4am to allow us to return to Bristol if things didn't improve. However, the wind had dropped and we only needed to pause for a couple of hours in Portishead Marina before the pilot said "GO" and we had left, with him on board, of course, arriving in Sharpness at 7pm. The elated team had enjoyed a quick meal together before Neil, Andrew and John had to summon up sufficient energy to undertake a several hour drive home! They had originally only planned to come from Bristol Harbour to Portishead Marina but, with the change in plans, had shuffled cars and come the whole way.

Neil, Alex' son, as the boat waited in Portishead Marina

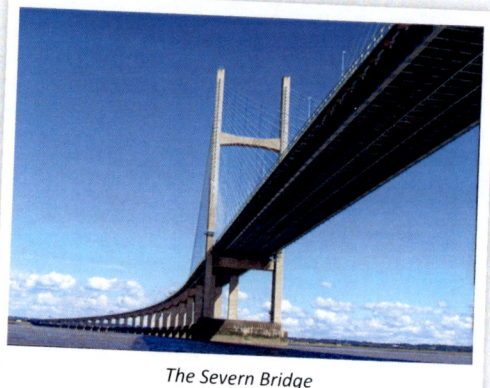

The Severn Bridge

Sharpness is so peaceful now, sadly much of the activity around the port has declined but for us that relaxing quiet meant visiting the Purton hulks, enjoying the wild beauty of the estuary countryside and even getting to Berkeley Castle by bus. We eventually travelled on up the Gloucester & Sharpness, stopping off at Peter Scott's Slimbridge Wetlands Centre and into Gloucester Docks.

After very strong winds, a wonderful break in the weather

From Gloucester we went up the Severn to Tewkesbury. The Severn continues on up to Worcester but that year we joined the River Avon which winds its way through Pershore and Evesham and on to Stratford. The Vale of Evesham, in the main, escaped the bombing of the Second World War and so the abbeys and churches are well preserved, along with other beautiful historic buildings. Stratford itself has excellent moorings complete with a little ferry across the river to the town and there is so much to see and do.

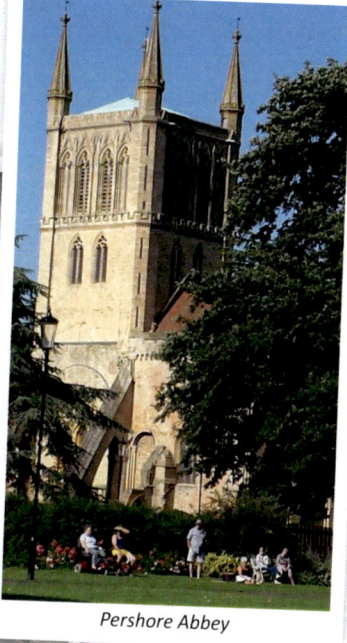

Pershore Abbey

Beautiful historic buildings in Evesham

Once up the Stratford Canal and the Birmingham & Fazeley Canals, we had reached the Midlands and the boat spent the winter on the Coventry Canal near Tamworth. When you pass through the Coventry, en route to other places, you never realise the beauty of that relatively flat area.

We had gradually worked our way up north and the boat spent the following two winters in Savile Wharf, Dewsbury. To get there we had to navigate the beautiful Macclesfield, the Peak Forest and then the very energetic Rochdale Canal. It's a great pity the Rochdale locks are such a challenge and the mooring unpredictable because the countryside is beautiful and the northern end goes up and over some amazing hills and through some steep sided ravines. Along the Rochdale and the Calder & Hebble we had reached Savile Wharf which was to be a useful base from which to explore York with the boat and to go on up to the Ripon Canal.

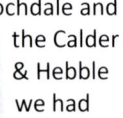

Autumn on the Coventry Canal

A steep ravine on the Rochdale Canal

I have to say going out on to the Ouse at Selby and coming back in are something I am glad I have done but not likely to repeat. Rivers all have their character but I had always made a point of venturing out on the bigger tidal waterways with a pilot on board, someone who knows the river's character and idiosyncrasies. On the Ouse the lockkeepers are wonderful and let you out at exactly the right time for the tide but navigating was entirely down to the private boater. Five rivers run down the surrounding hills and empty uncontrolled into the Ouse. This creates a very unpredictable situation, even in the summer. On the way up to Ripon the river rose up to four feet overnight with the accompanying enormous flow over the weirs and large pieces of flotsam and jetsam coming towards you. On the way back, on the contrary, it was like a pussy cat and we spent a wonderful weekend exploring York. The Ripon Canal, all three miles of it, was beautiful and had been a very welcome sanctuary from the changeable river. We had moored temporarily at the Race Course Marina at Ripon, fetched our car and explored this wonderful area, going as far as Barnard Castle and west to Swaledale.

One of the beautiful waterfalls on the Ingleton Trail near Carnforth

Ripon Cathedral

The Ice Cream Boat at York

A Boating Life

How to get to Liverpool

Over several years we have tried to go across the Mersey with a pilot and into Liverpool Dock. Before having the accident in 2013, I had planned that year to go into Liverpool but that obviously never happened. Alex and I both wanted to try again so in 2018 it was on that year's cruise document. The first change of plans was caused by the Middlewich Arm breach. OK, we said, we will go down on to the Weaver and go out through Marsh Lock and on to the Ship Canal to Ellesmere Port. We even obtained the certificate of seaworthiness required by Peel Ports. (You would think a current boat safety certificate would have sufficed but you need further paperwork for the Mersey.) We made all the necessary reservations for entry when coming across the Mersey and mooring with CRT in Salthouse dock. Before we descended to the Weaver on the Anderton Lift, we decided to explore the Runcorn Arm.

What is it they say? Life happens when you are making plans. One May Sunday morning we switched on the mobiles to find messages to ring Australia. My brother went out there to live several decades ago. This outwardly very healthy man had sat down in the car and died. We went to our sanctuary at Dutton Breach to absorb this overwhelmingly shocking news. Northwich Marina was wonderfully helpful and took care of the boat while we flew out to Sydney for John's funeral, still dazed by the events. It was no consolation at all but we were so thankful that we had flown out to Australia the year before, in 2017, and had wonderful times with John, his wife, Anne, and their grown up family.

Although going to Liverpool had somewhat paled into insignificance, on our return we thought we would try to rebook. However, uncannily in our absence the big trip boat, the Daniel Adamson, had badly damaged the lock gate at Marsh Lock, making exit on to the Ship Canal impossible. Alright we said to one another we will abandon yet again the idea of going across the Mersey and will go up the Bridgewater Canal and into the Liverpool Link from the north. Once again we booked our Salthouse berth and came up the Anderton Lift. As we did so the alert came through on my phone that the Leeds and Liverpool Canal had breached just north of the docks, making entry impossible! As you can imagine, at that point, we conceded defeat.

However, if we were to fast forward a year, Alex and I, accompanied by my brother–in- law from Australia, managed to travel along the canal from Leigh into Liverpool Dock and stay several days in the dock. To say we had a ball would be an understatement and a return visit is definitely on the cards. The scenery on the way, the people, the mooring and the different things to see and do were fantastic. As a sixties' child going to The Cavern was a very special occasion and we love live music. May be one day we will also manage to cross the Mersey in *About Time*. It's still on the plan.

Entering Liverpool on the Link

Moored so close to the centre in Salthouse

Based around Manchester

We had moved into the house in Oldham in 2015 and finally, in 2019, we started looking for an appropriate permanent marina for the boat and found Pennington Wharf at Leigh. Savile Town Wharf Marina had been super and staff and boaters very friendly but the Calder & Hebble and other waterways nearby were very weather dependent. They were often subject to the flood gates being closed, so boating could be unpredictable. Pennington was slightly closer to the house but it's main advantage was the long Bridgewater Canal, to the east, with no locks, and possible trips to Castlefield or further to the Trent & Mersey, or, to the west, the beautiful stretch of the Leeds & Liverpool Canal, with locks and swing bridges into Liverpool Dock. The Rufford Arm and the Wigan Flight, both going north, were also easily accessible. Grudgingly we had to acknowledge that we were not getting any younger, and nor were some of our friends, so a choice of cruising with or without locks was a bonus. Therefore, in August 2019, Pennington Wharf became *About Time's* permanent base.

Pennington Wharf Marina

On the Bridgewater Canal near Leigh

We have now explored a lot of the system together and will never tire of the changes provided by each canal or waterway. Sometimes it's stunning scenery and views, sometimes it's aqueducts and industrial buildings and even the different types of lock mechanisms! Oh, yes, and we've had to learn about handspikes.[12] On a canal like the Rochdale you often go past the old mill buildings. Many of them are protected but as you pass them you feel that you have turned the clock back a hundred years. The canals are changing places and so where the industrial buildings have been taken down often modern estates have sprung up. You also never imagine that in the UK you can be far away from a road but the canals, allowing for land contours, were built to transport products from port to city, town to town or factory to town. They crossed a lot of farm land and ridges and so as boaters we can sometimes find ourselves easily ten miles from the nearest shop or bus route, often a wonderful feeling in this modern world!

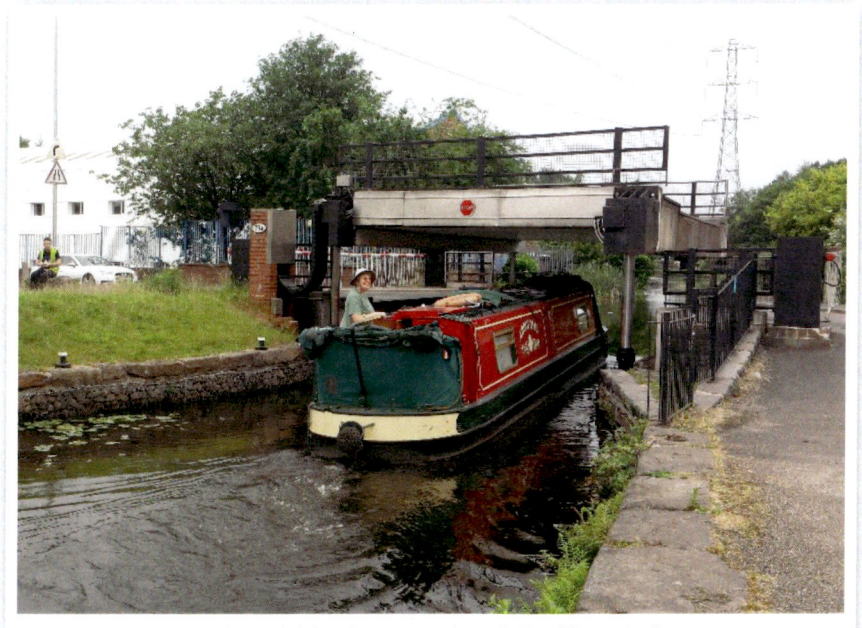

On the Rochdale. It's very rare that a bridge lifts vertically.

An old mill building, sometimes listed, and, therefore, often left to decay until demolition is essential.

The changing scenery is amazing. One minute you can be in a little village; the next climbing a lock flight; you can be going over an aqueduct as high as 125ft, 38 metres in new money, over the Pontcysyllte on the Llangollen or going through the 3000 yard Blisworth tunnel on the Grand Union. You are so close to nature and the seasons change the canals radically, from the blossoms and yellow irises (or flags) of spring, accompanied by the arrival of ducklings and other new life, to the wonderful autumn colours and the austere winter trees bereft of their leaves. We are always fascinated, too, that a canal or river can look so different when you travel in the opposite direction. It means you never tire of travelling the same waterway because there is always something different to see.

Going up and over hills means big locks!

Public awareness of the canals is so much greater in recent years and many others use the towpath or the water itself for relaxation and sport. You always acknowledge one another or stop to talk.

In years gone by the boats were purely for the transport of goods like clay, coal or stone, the whole family only living in a tiny back cabin. Occupying the whole boat for living would have been met with derision. However, another group of boaters now use the canal to trade. The Canal Traders provide anything from different foodstuffs to cleaning articles, or handmade articles. They might be a fender maker or a blacksmith. We have had delicious oatcakes, ice cream, Ecover products, jewellery, fenders and even a bespoke forged companion set from commercial boats and diesel, gas and coal from one of the remaining 14 licensed fuel boats. They have their own website and you can normally find these traders at the various boat rallies.

Paddleboarding on the Staffs & Worcester

You often experience nature's simple beauty from the boat

12 *Handspikes are actually a long piece of wood needed to open certain locks on the Calder & Hebble*

What next and Where next?

Boat maintenance always rears its ugly head, more so than in a house, partly because, with a steel narrowboat, you have to keep on top of the rust and a well running engine, too. We always have the boat serviced every year after the season. As we have been moving through the system, different engineers have taken on the task, some excellent, some not so good. Once at Savile Wharf we asked them to recommend someone. They said they would get him to ring us. Several days later the phone rang and David Omeroyd's name appeared on my mobile screen, the same engineer who had helped Elaine and myself after the accident in 2013! He now does all the maintenance on the boat and has taken over from Marcus and Patrick, so to speak.

Internally, we have recently changed curtains for roller blinds. So much lighter than curtains! The LED bulbs have an 8 year shelf life before they start going dimmer. No it's not our ageing eyesight! So they have been replaced recently too. Over the last few years we have had the bathroom revamped with plastic wall coverings and bifold doors. The latter is a great improvement in such a small space. Eventually the kitchen will need a similar rethink. I started out with carpeted floors but these have gradually been replaced by laminate flooring, which is so practical, and, with insulation beneath, it is still warm and cosy.
We have also changed the chemical toilet for a composting toilet which is a reasonable step forward. On the one side it is much more practical but CRT has yet to provide a separate disposal bin. We still wouldn't change back.

Looking at the outside of the boat, we now always take the boat to Burton for its triannual blacking because they use a steam jet, not a cold water one, to clean the hull and the finish is so much better. We have taken on all the "green painting" ourselves and have replaced the deck green and chimney areas with Hammerite. The red presents a problem, however, as it fades so fast and, of course, there are the graphics on the sides. So hoping that we may have a better solution, financially and for durability, we are having the sides painted and varnished and the hatch and locker tops powder coated this year. After these processes we should only have to have the sides revarnished every three to four years. So April 2021 will see us taking the boat up the Leeds & Liverpool to Tony and Craig at Barnoldswick. Of course, we like the boat to look good but we are not forever polishing and cleaning. We use it a lot and any work is more to protect it from the knocks and the weather.

We want to go on exploring for many a year, health permitting. In 2020, boating was a godsend. You could be out in nature and yet stay safe. Going across the Mersey with a pilot is one ambition but friends have recently bought a house in Ely and Alex' time with his cruiser was spent on the Great Ouse. He would like to go back. So once the boat painting has been finished in April, we are off down the Bridgewater Canal. It'll take us a couple of months and involve the Trent & Mersey, the Coventry, the north Oxford and the Grand Union and, finally, up the locks at Northampton and into East Anglia. The boat will be away from its home mooring for several months and for a short while we will be nearer lots of friends and family.

We have always loved sharing the boating with friends and family and obviously want to continue to do so. In 2021 the boat will come back to Pennington Wharf around September or October and hope Manchester friends will join us for day trips. The planned day trips of 2020, obviously, never happened. That's this year's plan but we hope there will be many more adventures to come, exploring the several thousand miles which make up the UK inland waterways!

Lots of wonderful towpath picnics - Maureen, Jean and Bruce

Fun on the lock. Harry, Darcey and my grandson, Joshua

Recently on the Rufford Arm with Rebecca and Debs

Tidal rivers
Broad canals
Narrow canals
Planned or canals under restoration
MANCHESTER
BIRMINGHAM
LONDON
BORWICK
RIPON
River Ouse
River Derwent
YORK
Lancaster Canal
Leeds & Liverpool Canal
LEEDS
BLACKBURN
BURNLEY
PRESTON
HULL
River Hull
Rochdale Canal
HUDDERSFIELD
DONCASTER
WIGAN
Manchester Ship Canal
LIVERPOOL
Bridgewater Canal
SHEFFIELD
River Trent
River Ancholme
LINCOLN
River Witham Navigation
Fossdyke Navigation
River Dee
STOKE
NOTTINGHAM
BOSTON
Trent & Mersey Canal
Grantham Canal
River Welland & Glen
LEICESTER
Grand union Canal
PETERBOROUGH
River Wissey
Little Ouse River
River Nene
Middel Level Navigation
COVENTRY
STOURPORT
NORTHAMPTON
River Lark
WORCESTER
STRATFORD
River Cam
BEDFORD
CAMBRIDGE
River Severn
River Avon
MILTON KEYNES
SUDBURY
River Stour
Monmouthshire and Breakon Canal
TEWKSBURY
Grand union Canal
BISHOP'S STORTFORD
COLCHESTER
HERTFORD
River Stort
GLOUCESTER
OXFORD
CHELMSFORD
River Lee & Stort
River Crouch
River Roach
River Thames
Grand Union Canal
River Thames
BRISTOL
READING
River Avon
WOKING
Wey & Godalming Navigation
MAIDSTONE
BATH
Kennet & Avon Canal
NEWBURY
GUILDFORD
River Medway
Basingstoke Canal
TONBRIDGE
River Parret
GODALMING
Wey & Arun Canal
Bridgewater & Taunton Canal
TAUNTON
River Rother
River Arun

My boat with an on board garden. Lockdown definitely increased the horticulture!